To Sasha

Now and forever,
my heart is yours

Table of Contents

Dear Friends,

Thank you for purchasing this book.

You are entering a new era. An era in which you are in control of what happens inside your own body. **Yes. Did that make sense?**

Read it again. YOU ARE IN CONTROL. Not anyone else. When you are in control, you are also responsible for your own actions. With the great freedom comes the great burden of making the right choices in relation to your health. The aim of this book is to give you tried and tested practical tips on how to reduce the likelihood of causing an injury in your own home and thus providing you with tools to enhancing, rather than hindering your health.

I was compelled to write this book; I simply could not sit on my hands any longer. I had to write this down and make It available to you else I explode. See, over the years in practice I have noticed that most people do not have the basic knowledge on how to operate their bodies. These observations were borne from sheer repetition of the same problems bashing me in the face and in the end I saw the patterns. In this book I will try and convey some of the lessons learned the hard way, so you don't have to.

I am a chiropractor by profession and by training. I am also a very curious person. I have had this nagging feeling that something is missing and that I am missing something in my daily practise. Sure, people are getting better and people are staying better, but still. I have been feeling incomplete. Like I was not fulfilling my role to the best of my ability.

In this book, you will receive basic instructions to operating the human body. Don't get me wrong, the complete user manual is a huge thing, and this ebook is only the first volume, but just absorbing these guidelines into your life will greatly enhance your ability to move in a good and functional manner. It will make you aware of the various aspects of your daily life and help you make them work for you, rather than against you.

Enjoy.

Movement Revolution

I grew up in rural Finland. Lots of my time was spent outdoors playing, running, and climbing in the forest. I played lots of sport throughout my educational years and lapsed into a bit of a sedentary life as I started work. True enough, I was busy, tired, and preoccupied - sport and exercise were the last things on my mind. There were a few wakeup calls that nudged me in the right direction along the way. My weight climbed up to a level that I was not comfortable with, hence I joined a gym. The gym was not getting me any results and it was doing my head in, hence I quit the gym and started to run. The running hurt, hence I figured that I had to learn to run better. After my forays into many different sports I still felt incomplete. I searched for inspiration in various different places and often got close only to realise that in a way I was again further from the truth. Then my kids were born. As I witnessed them struggling to learn the very basics of movement and function I felt something shift inside of me. My eyes literally popped open at that point. It was a whole new way of looking at life and movement. I was able to learn through their experience and I was left speechless by their sheer tenacity and willingness to learn. I became fascinated by the way they moved and by the way they learned to move. I started to think small and went back to studying the basics of physiology and neurology. This time (after University) I had a different appreciation and a new pair of eyes on the text, so to speak. All of a sudden it made a lot more sense.

The journey of a thousand miles begins with a single step.

Fast forward a couple of years. My girls have learned to walk, to swim, to ride a bike, to run. Now their lives are an incessant gymnastics class. They spend so much time being upside down or sideways, running or sliding, climbing or crawling, that it simply puts every grown up to shame. The amount of variety of movement in their daily activities is bewildering. For them it's entirely natural. Why would you want to sit down to eat, if you can do it while crab walking over the side of the sofa? Why would you want to stand still to clean your teeth, if you can do it pretending to cross a river of hungry crocodiles (simulated by the bath tub)? Why would you want to sit down to watch telly, if you can do something else? Movement is an expression of life! It is a way to feel alive!

I personally realised that trying to learn to keep up with my girls, I would have to go back to the basics as well. I had to get fitter and stronger, but equally I had to learn to move in an organic manner, in which injuries do not occur and I am able to utilise my body to my best ability. I had to become fearless again. See, for young kids there is only success. The success is inevitable and they will learn it. The number of failed attempts is entirely inconsequential and each near-success only fuels the fire and the desire to try again. They have no fear because they are not worried about failing. They are not self conscious of 'looking silly' or not 'acting their age' or other nonsense. There is a lot for us all to learn.

The sooner you get started, the sooner you get there.

I learned about gymnastics. I learned about parkour and capoeira. I learned about break dancing (I am a rubbish dancer still). I learned about climbing. I learned about running and cycling and swimming and all manner of other movement. Until I realised that it has all been compiled into a 'thing' already. Guys like Ido Portal, Erwan le Corre and Mike Fitch have been doing this same work for years. I was happy to take on their teachings as well and to further develop my own ideas. They all refer to it as the "movement revolution". It is a revolution simply because it goes against the normal. Nowadays kids and grownups alike are heavily discouraged from exploring and enjoying movement. Seeing someone climbing trees, slacklining or even doing cartwheels in the park is generally frowned upon, and most people would feel obliged to call the police if one was to encourage kids to join in. But that is about to change. There is a shift towards movement and getting out of the artificial concept of "fitness" and the modern false paradigm of "health" prescribed by The Powers That Be as more and more people are simply starting to do what they feel is right, and most importantly, what makes them happy.

> Running injuries are caused by running, and running injuries are cured by running – **correctly.**

Go back to the very basics. Start from the beginning. Walk before you run - go the old sayings. Does that sound familiar? That's how most things are being taught. For some reason one always assumes that their basics are sound. One assumes that they are well beyond the beginning, thus running and leaping are definitely on the agenda. They are wrong. I would argue that most people would greatly benefit from relearning to crawl, to stand and so forth. But this time doing it properly. With a clear understanding of what they are trying to learn.

The problem with movement is that it relies on proprioception (subconscious feedback of sensory information to the brain), which is influenced by all of the previous injuries and bad habits that may be hindering one's ability to accurately feel what one's body is doing. Rewiring the brain will take a while, but restoring factory setting and then re-learning from the beginning are really the only way one can pull this off. Don't be insulted. I am not saying that all that you have done until now is wrong and bad. I am saying that now is the time to get out of your own way and to learn things properly.

A long time ago someone told me that **running injuries are caused by running, and running injuries are cured by running – correctly**. This made me think at the time, and even more so now. Because it is true. This is beautiful, since it also takes away the modern affliction of expecting an instant external cure. The human body and brain require time to heal. Thus, taking the time and reducing expectations is vital in order to allow the brain enough time to compute the new requirements and to create adaptation to meet the new requirements. The journey is long. It can be difficult and frustrating at times. There are moments when you will question your motives and going back to the old way seems so much easier. But. BUT! You will continue. Because you owe it to yourself. Because it is the only way that makes sense. Going back to the blinkered and numb existence of mindless ignorance is already impossible. By having read this far, I have already succeeded in planting a seed in your brain. This seed will grow and slowly take root. Some people will embrace it and grow rapidly, some will resist and deny it – they will struggle. Until, one day they will finally have had enough of the pain and injuries, the constant feeling of discomfort that comes from suppressing the very basic nature of one's' being. I know they will.

I Challenge You!

> At this point, I guess, I should throw you a challenge. A rousing glimpse of what might be. Something to work towards and something that would make your daily commitment to your own improvement worth your while.

I challenge you to remember your wildest dreams. Yes, those ones that you never made a reality.

Climbing mountains

sailing the seas

riding horses

scuba diving

anything...

See, we all have (or had) these dreams. Things that we thought: **"that would be absolutely awesome to do"**, or **"achieving that would make me feel like a million bucks"**... Stuff that we let go and forgot due to lack of ability/money/time/support/permission/fitness/strength/opportunity. In other words, there was always an excuse for not chasing our dreams.

Well now it's time to get back to your dreams and make them come true. Nobody will do it for you. Nobody will live your life and make your decisions but you. A dream becomes a goal when you commit to the idea. A goal becomes a target when you formulate a plan and stick to it. Simple.

Now sit down in your favorite place and take 10 minutes to simply think of all the awesome and fun experiences you will achieve.

Your daily routine – potion or poison?

What do you do each day? What percentage of your day is spent sitting, standing, walking, lying down, or doing other movement? Write it down. It's pretty easy. Each hour in your day is about 4%. You can either do a rough estimate by the hour or go down to as fine a detail as you like.

For example, my typical Monday is: sleep 24%, sitting down 20%, standing and walking 20%, work (combination of stand, walk, sit, move) 24%, other movement (playing with kids, cycling to commute, toilet, shower etc) 12%. Most people will find a very different breakdown. The typical breakdown may be something like: Sleep 36%, sitting down 52%, walking 6%, other stuff (that may or may not include specific exercise) 6%.

What I am trying to get to with this little exercise is that in order for you to get somewhere, you must first understand where you are starting from. Setting targets is impossible without knowing your starting parameters.

As far as changing your daily routine is concerned, I know there are lots of things that can not be changed. Most of us have to go to work. Most of us have to sleep. Most of us need to drive to places and sit down for meals. Yet the way we do these things can be changed. Instead of simply plopping your bottom in the seat and just mindlessly expecting the chair to support you, why don't you sit up in a mindful manner, where you are seeking to optimise your body alignment and positioning so that your sitting becomes a part of the solution rather than a part of the problem?

The same principle can be applied to most other daily activities, such as cleaning your teeth, doing household chores, the walk at school drop off and pick up, even taking out the rubbish can be used as a part of your 'workout' – if you pay attention. If you are going to be doing it anyway, you might as well get some benefit from it, right?

Here is the rub. Most of us have no idea how to operate the body. A bold statement, I know. But seriously, how many of us are aware of the fact that there are numerous different ways to pick things up from the floor? How many of us have ever tried a few different variations?

What I am proposing is very different. It is a way to put you firmly into the driver's seat and start regaining control of your body - maybe for the first time in your life. It doesn't matter if you are young or old, fit or fat, athletic or a slouch, we all start from somewhere and work our way from there. But, by applying the following principles you will improve your ability to be aware of your body, you will learn the difference between good and bad movement patterns, and you will be well on your way to creating a resilient and injury proof body.

EXERCISE 1 Starting Line

- *Write down your typical weekday breakdown. Start by writing down your hourly schedule and then add up your total hours of each activity. Finally calculate the percentages by multiplying the hours by 4.167. As you know your starting point, you can then set goals to increase variety in your days.*

EXERCISE 2 Adding Variety

- *Try different variations of your everyday activities. Be creative. This can be applied to anything. Sit on the floor to watch TV. Take the stairs instead of the lift. Pick things up from the floor by not bending your spine. Get up from the bed or from sitting on the floor by not using your hands. The list is endless. Have fun exploring. For best effect, either make a video montage or simply write it down.*

Anatomical Neutral

In order for this book to make any practical sense, let's start by defining the desired starting point. Now, some of you may actually have trouble getting to the starting position due to injuries or ailments, but don't despair - you can still apply the lessons in this book to your best ability and gain benefit, or visit us at the clinic to find out how we can get you there.

Anatomical Neutral is the natural standing position of the human body, where everything is relaxed and aligned. Most of us are deviated from this to such a degree that it feels very strange to arrange yourself in a well aligned position. In the anatomical neutral the spinal curve is normal, the levels of ears, shoulders and hips are even, the chest is open and the abdomen is flat. Legs are relaxed but bouncy and the arms rest by your sides.

Benefits of anatomical neutral posture include:

Neutral Spine good alignment, reduced strain on the vertebrae and discs, free flow of neural impulses along the spinal cord and spinal nerves.

Open Chest free breath, ability to costal breathe, reduced tightness in the diaphragm and intercostal muscles.

Upright Position of Neck and Head reduced strain on the neck muscles and upper back vertebrae, reduced likelihood of headaches and migraines.

Flat abdomen combined with full breathing will enhance digestive health and gut motility, better ability to utilise and to coordinate the Core muscles.

Level shoulders and hips reduced strain in the muscles and from the spine.

Relaxed legs greater balance, less fatigue, reduction of muscle imbalances and strain, better gait mechanics.

EXERCISE 3 The Anatomical Neutral (AN) Position

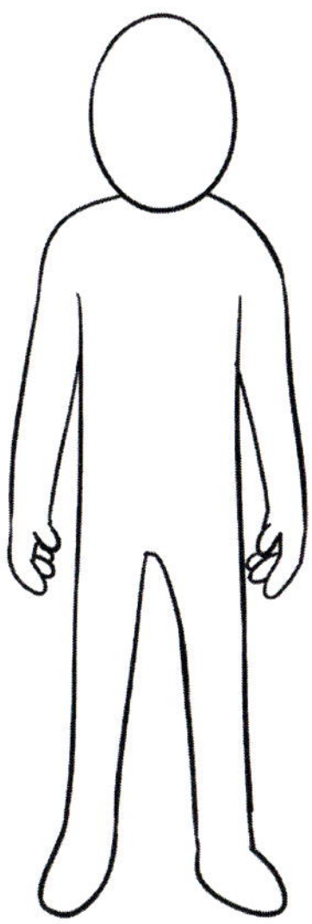

- *Start by aligning your feet flat on the floor and square to each other, about hip width apart.*
- *Soften the ankles and knees. No locking back. Bounce a bit – feel the elasticity of the legs.*
- *Slightly engage the bottom part of your buttock muscles, this will rotate your hip joints out and almost thrust your pelvis forward a fraction.*
- *Lift your sternum. Not by inflating your chest, simply by engaging the muscles around the lower back and abdomen.*
- *At this point you will notice that the very bottom most part of your abdominals, a muscle called Pyramidalis activates. This muscle sits behind the belt buckle and right in front of your body's centre of gravity.*
- *Allow your shoulders to fall backwards as a result of the lifting of the sternum. Don't pull the shoulders back, simply let them drop into their allocated positions.*
- *Position your head in between your shoulders if it's not already there. You have to slightly engage the deeper muscles in the front of the neck, or throat to get to this position.*
- *If you have a mirror in front of you, you should notice perfect levelling of the eyes, ears, shoulders, hips and the knees. On the side view the ears, shoulders, hips, knees, and ankles should all line up.*

That feels pretty good, right?

Anatomical Neutral

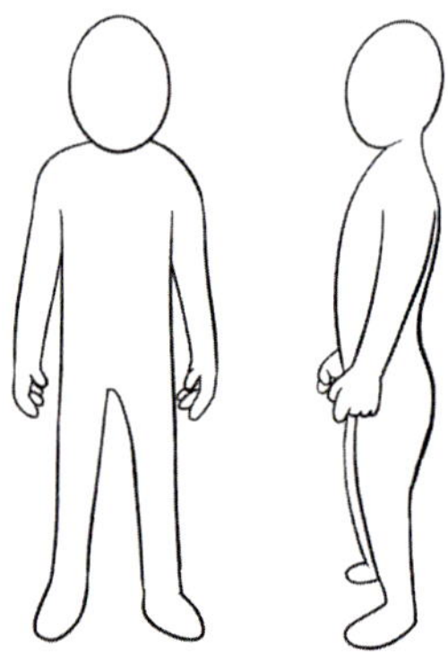

The Anatomical Neutral position (AN) will be referred to a lot in this book so please learn it well. Spend a bit of time standing in front of the mirror to check your position. Close your eyes and allow the feedback from your body to flood your brain. Noticing the various signals from your body will help your brain understand what you are trying to achieve. You can perform this Standing Meditation a few times a day for a minute or so at a time as you start learning. It will greatly speed up the process of rewiring your brain. As you get better holding the AN, and the standing meditation will become easier and you only need to do it once per day to remind yourself.

Stoop

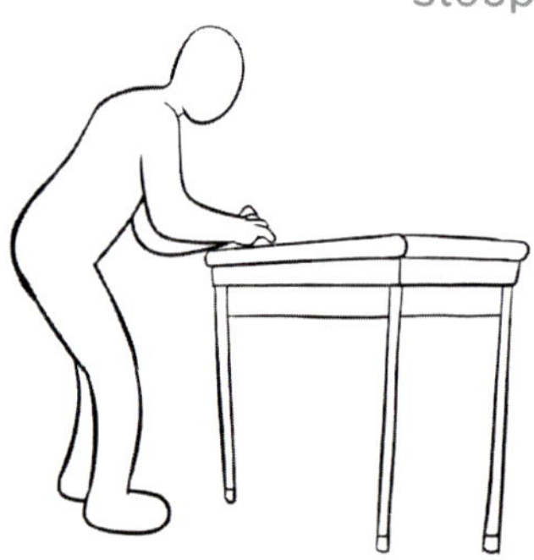

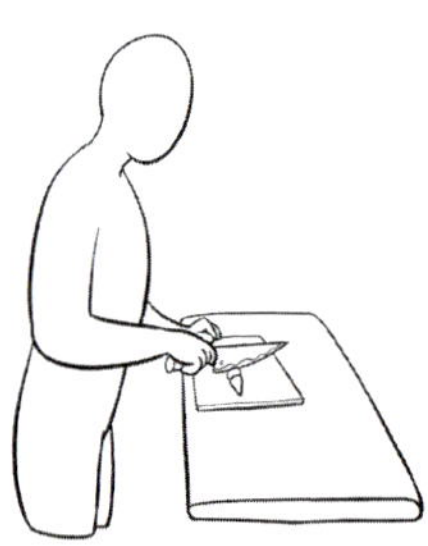

AN is the starting point to all movement and activity. In the beginning, it may be helpful to first assume AN and think how you can get into the position that you need with as little deviation from AN as possible, or how the required movements can be performed by maintaining as much of AN as possible. The maintenance of the trunk position, or spinal angle, is always primary, and must be the last one compromised.

There are multiple variations on this simple theme that can be easily adopted to get into appropriate positions for the different tasks around the house.

The stoop is to be used instead of bending down from the spine. This involves a start from the AN and moving the trunk forward by flexion of the hips and knees as and when necessary. Most useful applications include: cleaning teeth, chopping food in the kitchen.

High Kneeling

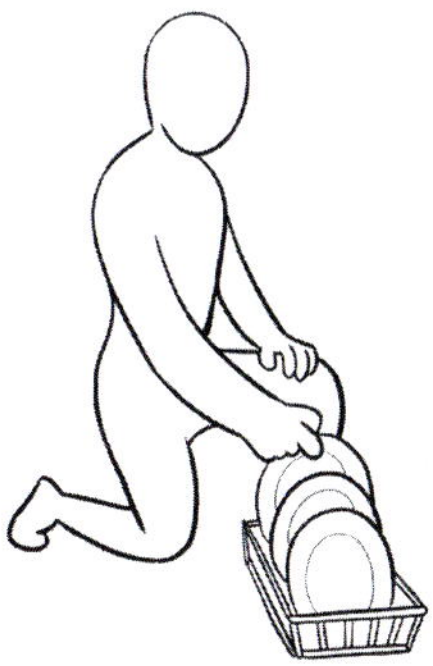

The high kneeling position is good when you need to get down to a relatively low height for a longer time. Start from AN, bring one knee onto the floor and the other leg flexed in front, or to the side of you, with hip and knee at right angles. The trunk will remain upright again. A fantastic position for emptying the dishwasher.

The four point kneeling position is best utilised when the need is to get down to floor level for a longer time. This time both knees and hands are on the floor. The body is supported with a straight spine at horizontal, this enables you to balance well and to utilise the core muscles to protect your midsection. From here scrubbing and weeding become much less strenuous.

Four Point Kneeling

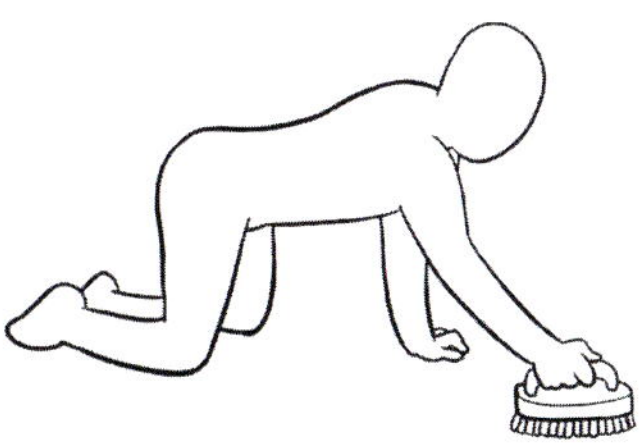

The modified Martial Arts stance is essentially the human elevator movement. Starting with AN, widen and open your stance a bit by turning one foot outward. Now maintaining your mid section activation and spinal angle you can lower yourself down significantly by bending the hips and the knees into a squat position. The static version can easily be used when lifting, or pulling the bin bag out of the bin.

Modified Martial Arts

> The maintenance of the trunk position, or spinal angle, is always primary, and must be the last one compromised.

Deep Squat

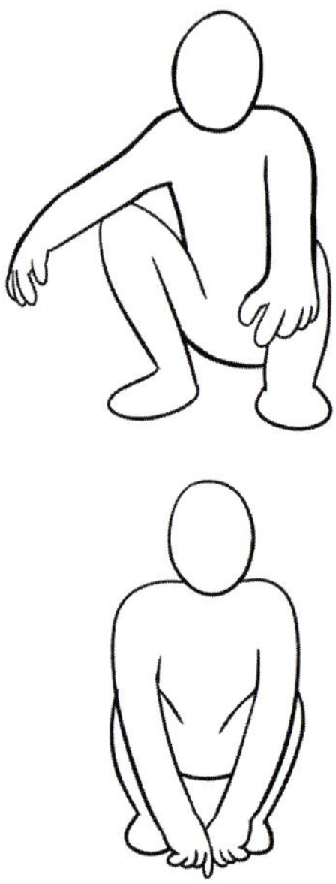

The mobile version is fantastic for hoovering, when you simply move your body weight from one foot to the other and back again. This eliminates the need for trunk flexion again.

The deep squat is a great mobiliser. Lots of people struggle to get into the deep squat to begin with, but with practise it becomes one of the most comfortable positions to assume when working on something low down. Start again from AN, simply bend the legs until your bottom nearly touches the floor. You need to tuck your tail under towards the end of the movement, but this is fine. At the bottom of the movement your legs should still remain in straight alignment and your feet should still be pointing forward. If this is not the case, please utilise a bannister or similar to hold onto as you lower yourself down as this will help with the mechanics and ensure better technique.

Cross Legs

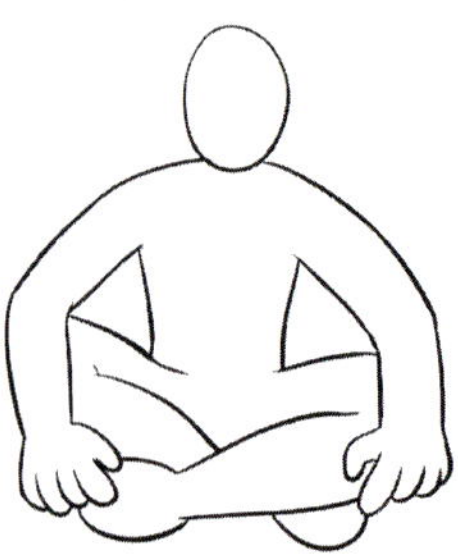

The cross legged sitting position is great for watching the TV, reading, meditating and even working on the laptop. Of course, to follow on the theme from earlier, maintaining the spinal angle and uprightness of the trunk is important, and it may take time and practise for you to be able to relax in this position. It is a good hip opener.

EXERCISE 4 Alternative Position

Go through the list above and revise the various body positions. Try and apply each one of them to different tasks in and around the house. You will soon realise which positions are suited for given tasks and which are not.

ANATOMICAL NEUTRAL

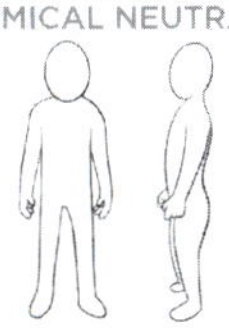

HOUSEHOLD ACTIVITY 1

HOUSEHOLD ACTIVITY 2

STOOP

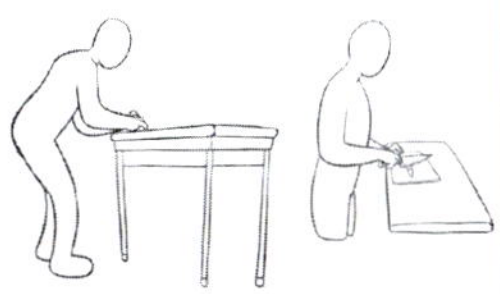

HOUSEHOLD ACTIVITY 1

HOUSEHOLD ACTIVITY 2

HIGH KNEELING

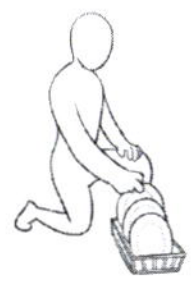

HOUSEHOLD ACTIVITY 1

HOUSEHOLD ACTIVITY 2

FOUR POINT KNEELING

HOUSEHOLD ACTIVITY 1

HOUSEHOLD ACTIVITY 2

MODIFIED MARTIAL ARTS

HOUSEHOLD ACTIVITY 1

HOUSEHOLD ACTIVITY 2

DEEP SQUAT

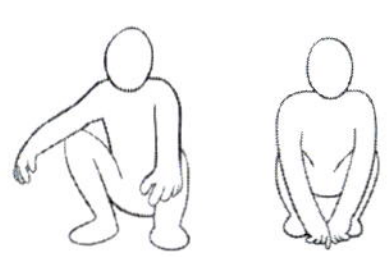

HOUSEHOLD ACTIVITY 1

HOUSEHOLD ACTIVITY 2

CROSS LEGS

HOUSEHOLD ACTIVITY 1

HOUSEHOLD ACTIVITY 2

Sleeping

Sleeping is an important part of our lives. Most of us tend to spend anywhere between 5 and 11 hours in bed per night, with the average near the 8 hour mark. When anything is done for that period of time, with such frequency, technique becomes important. A good sleeping position is vital as it allows you to have a good restful sleep and it will help you recover from the stress and strain of the day. The night time exists precisely for this reason, to allow the body a chance to repair and to regenerate (the rotation of the earth and its orbit around the sun are merely convenient coincidences, of course).

Most people tend to lie on their side. Yet by 'side' they generally mean semi-prone, as in mostly on their front. One leg is characteristically extended straight, with the other one bent up to a certain degree. Usually people combine this with lying either on the tip of the shoulder or slightly more on the front of the shoulder, with one arm in front of the face and the other behind the back. Some like to have a pillow under the chest. Usually people have one to three pillows under the head.

If you recognise yourself from the example above, or confess to sleeping on your front, please read the following carefully.

There are generally speaking two very good ways to sleep. Either on your back, or CORRECTLY on your side.

When sleeping on the back, you must arrange yourself in a comfortable manner onto the mattress. You should place a couple of cushions under your knees, to allow the legs to be slightly bent. This will eliminate the strain from the legs, the hips, and the tummy as well as allow the back to rest on the mattress. As you rest your head onto the pillow, grab a hold of the corners of the pillow and gently drag the pillow down so that the corners rest on top of your shoulders. This will create a cradle for your head that will stop any jerky movements of the head if you are dreaming, as well as a slight roll under your neck that will support the normal curve of your neck. Arrange your arms either by the sides or on your chest - avoid the tummy as the weight of the hands may become uncomfortable.

When sleeping on your side the best position is the so called foetal position. Here you draw your knees fairly high up with a pillow or a thick cushion between them, which allows your legs to remain parallel and your pelvis to stay square in relation to the legs, easing the sprain in the pelvic joints. As your pelvis is square and your back lies straight, the rotation that often tightens up the low back muscles is removed. As you position yourself onto your shoulder blade (not on the tip of the shoulder), you will have a larger contact area with the mattress and therefore a more stable position which allows the muscles of the shoulder girdle, upper back, and neck to relax. This also removes one of the potential causes of shoulder impingement syndrome, or supraspinatus tendinitis from the equation. As the distance from the head to the mattress is reduced, you will again feel more comfortable with one pillow.

Sleeping on the back, or correctly on the side, not only has a biomechanical advantage over any other way, but seems to improve sleep quality as well. It is a natural progression that as the body is more comfortable, the mind is more at ease. Learning to sleep in a different position is not the easiest task in the world, but rest assured, that all it takes is practice. After a while replacing the pillows into their respective places if they have moved during the night becomes second nature and you may not even fully awaken to do it.

Other ways of improving your sleep quality include reducing your caffeine intake in the latter part of the day, ensuring sufficient physical and mental tiredness, listening to a binaural beat recording or a relaxation tape before bed time, reducing the amount of exposure to blue light in the bedroom and after sunset. In cases of more severe insomnia certain supplements and even hypnotherapy can be very helpful.

If you are a self-confessed front sleeper this change may be relatively difficult to make. I personally have been able to get there and I used a neat little trick - a cuddle pillow. By holding a pillow over your chest when lying on your back or on the side you simulate the sensation of pressure on the chest that most of front sleepers find very comfortable, hence you can trick your brain into thinking that you are in your old comfy front sleeping position. Over time the need for the cuddle pillow becomes less and less and you can probably discard it entirely after a while.

Getting out of bed is another skill to learn. A lot of people tend to perform a sit-up and move along from there. I would like to discourage that option as this places great strain on the pelvic and lower spine structures before you have even had the opportunity to wake up properly. The best technique of getting out of bed is to roll onto the side, as described above, and then get into a sitting position by simultaneously swinging the legs out of bed and the upper body up by pushing off the bed with you hand.

The question of mattress and pillow

This is something I get asked about virtually on a daily basis. What is the best mattress and which pillow should I buy? I guess the answer is: The one you get on with the best. Unhelpful, I know. But realistically I cannot give a universal recommendation on the best mattress or pillow because we are all different and we all have different preferences. I can say that from my chiropractic point of view the best combination would be the firmest choice one can handle. A firm bed in combination with good body positioning will allow for the best quality rest as the body will be able to settle down and rest. If the bed is too soft then the body will be constantly shifting and tightening muscles to ensure good positioning, which leads to reduced recovery in the night time and increases soreness and stiffness in the morning.

The most cost effective way of determining whether it is time get a new mattress or if the mattress is too soft is to simply sleep on the floor a few nights. Make your bed on the floor with a spare duvet and be mindful of your positioning when lying down. If you feel much better in the morning you know it is time to make the investment. If however there is no difference or you are left feeling even worse, then chances are that your problems lie not in the bed but in the body. When it comes to making the purchase, most bed companies operate a ' 30-day trial' scheme, by which you can 'test sleep' the mattress at home for a while to ensure comfort and satisfaction - makes sure you ask for that option.

EXERCISE 5 Revitalise your sleep

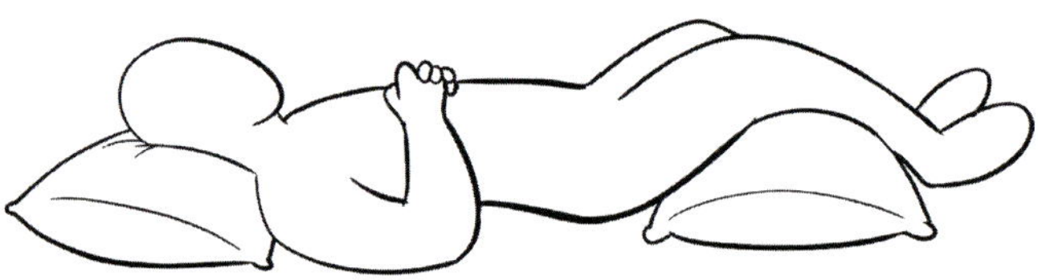

- *Adopt a good sleeping position. Have your partner, parent or friend check your positioning and correct it as necessary. Getting into good habits early on is very important. Then simply persevere. This may take a little while to get used to but it will definitely be worth it as you learn to recover better at night. When turning over at night it is a good idea to rouse yourself enough to replace the pillows and cushions into their proper places in case they have fallen out of position. After a while this will happen more or less automatically and you will not even notice doing it.*

Sitting

Sitting down constitutes a large proportion of our days, and it's killing us. We sit down at work, for the commute, for driving, meals, to watch TV, to read, on the loo etc. Our lives have become very sedentary and it shows. Illnesses and ailments rooted in inactivity have become the biggest killers and it looks like it's only going to get worse.

In my opinion there is a way to stop this. It's very simple and logical - almost too logical to be credible. Sit down less. Use your imagination, pretend the chairs do not exist, and go about your day in the normal way. You will quickly notice how redundant the chairs actually are.

But in case you still insist on sitting, then allow me to give you a few tips on how to reduce the damage and potentially even turn it into something, if not positive, then at least neutral in its effect on your health and body. It again requires a slight shift in your thinking. You must replace sitting down with sitting UP! I will explain.

Imagine a soldier standing at attention or at ease. Now imagine that soldier doing the same but in a sitting position. YES! Very little actually has changed. Only he has flexed his knees and hips. He is still very close to his anatomical neutral, but instead of his weight resting on his legs, it is now on his sitting bones. He is still able to maintain perfect spine angle and openness of his chest and abdomen. He is not compressing his discs, his lungs or his other organs, nor is he placing great strain onto his neck by jutting his head forward. He is well aligned and hence he is efficient. This position will be helpful as it maintains the principle of Anatomical Neutral (AN) beautifully.

EXERCISE 6 Sitting up

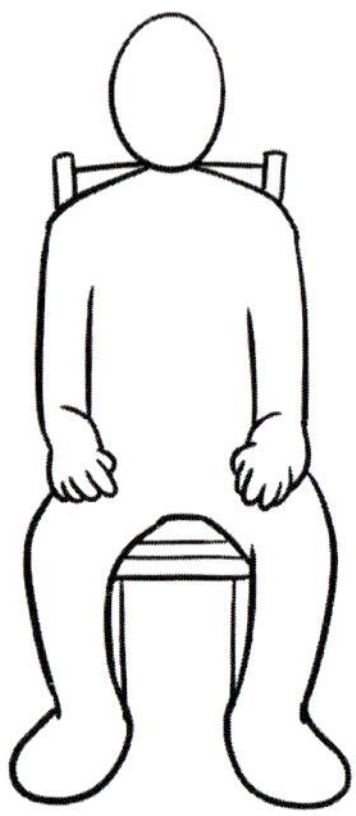

As you go to sit down into a chair push yourself into the image of the soldier. In order to be upright you need to focus on three things.

1) Tilt your pelvis forward so that your tummy is sticking out (pelvic neutral)

2) lift your sternum to square up your shoulders and to elongate your spine

3) place your head in between your shoulders (if it's not already there). You will notice that sitting like this requires very little effort and no contact with the backrest of the chair.

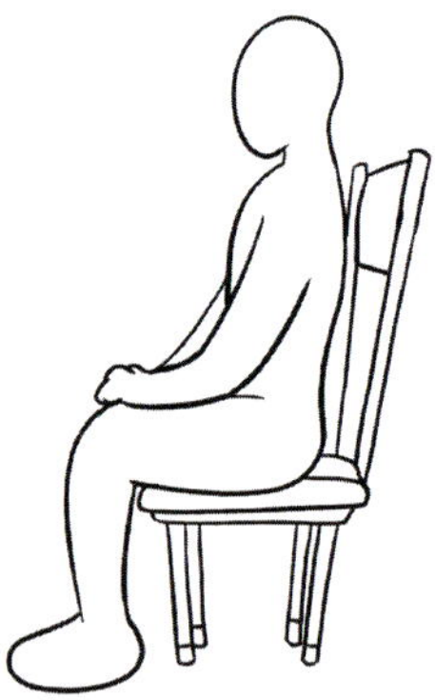

Most importantly, you should always try and sit as tall as you possibly can - Remember that sitting position is 90% reliant on the person to do it right, not the seat.

Let's take the above soldier and make his recline. Again, very little has to change. It is simply an extension at the hip joints. Not the spine. Correct, you read that right. You recline by reducing the flexion at the hip joint, while maintaining the angle of the spine and pelvis. This results in a gap between your low back and the seat. That is fine. It only becomes problematic when you allow your low back to bend and mould into the seat. You may wish to fill this natural gap with cushions, but after a while of doing this you will notice that you will no longer need them, as your body is content to support itself. I know, this is highly unusual. It is ok to relax and recline. But try and not to slouch - that's what puts tremendous strain on the low back and the pelvis.

Sitting - How not to do it

Let's go through a few choice examples of how not to do it (I won't name and shame). Many people will recognise themselves from one or more of the following descriptions:

1) *Sitting leaning onto the arm rest, with legs tucked to the side of you - often, neck is rotated in the opposite direction to gaze into the telly. After a while you will notice the unpleasant tightening of the muscles around the sides which will later intensify into a more urgent burning sensation. Most people choose to ignore the danger signs.*

2) *Leaning back and sliding down until only your bum is touching the front edge of the sofa and your shoulders and neck are touching the cushion at the back - spine slumped down. This one is the archetypical slumper posture. If you are on the market for a chronic low back problem, then this is the posture of choice!*

3) *Semi cross-legged sitting, one leg tucked under the bum, the other dangling in front. Crouching down to work on a laptop is optional (yet frequently observed). This kind of asymmetry is good for developing muscular imbalances and joint restrictions, especially around the hips.*

4) *Sitting somewhat upright, with legs crossed at the knee - sometimes with the legs tilted to one side to maximise the twisting of the pelvis and lumbar spine. This is an all time favorite for the ladies. Pelvic sprain is pretty much a certainty after a while.*

5) *Lying down on back of the sofa, wedged in between the armrests, with neck jammed into full flexion against the armrest as the legs are too long to comfortably fit in the sofa - you may require help from someone with a crowbar to be able to get out of this position. Needless to say, a jolly old neck injury is relatively certain and may even come with a headache and dizziness. Sometimes the lower neck injury may even produce neurological symptoms into the arms.*

6) *Side lying, with head propped up with five cushions and one leg on the armrest, the other twisted over so that the knee is resting on the floor - unable to get off the sofa as both arms have gone numb. Here the spine is rotated as far as it goes. As a yoga pose, held for a minute it is probably not too bad, but if maintained for any length of time, it soon becomes problematic.*

7) *The case of a seriously soft sofa - as you sit down, it feels like your bum is sinking through the floor, so that you end up with your knees sticking up in front of your face. It may take several attempts to get out, as you need to build up momentum by rocking back and forward to finally launch yourself up and into freedom, provided your low back has not completely seized up and you are still capable of any kind of movement.*

Needless to say - not one of the previous examples is very good for you, as all place excessive strain onto the body either through twisting, compressing or due to lack of support. The human body is very badly designed for sitting, yet in the modern world most of us spend ever increasing hours sat down. There are a few important check points that will reduce the likelihood of causing yourself mischief whilst sat down.

Sitting - Best Seat in the House

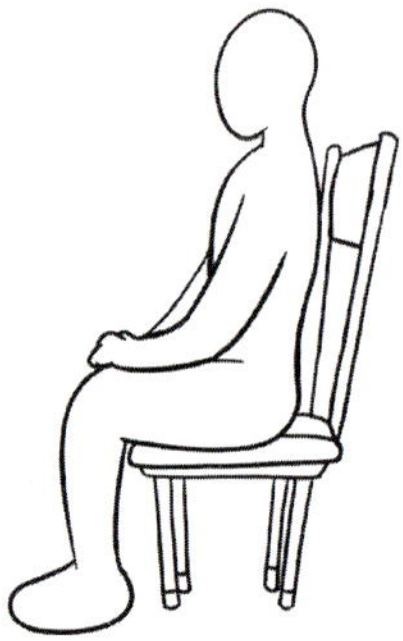

The best seat in the house is probably the dining room chair. I know, not the luxurious leather "lazy boy" arm chair. A couple of guidelines when choosing the best seat in the house below.

1) *Seat height should allow you to sit with your feet resting flat on the floor and with your knees below the level of the hips.*

2) *Seat depth should let you comfortably rest your back against the backrest with your bum tucked into the fold of the seat and with your legs resting down with bent knees.*

3) *The seat as well as the backrest should be firm and supportive.*

Most importantly, you should always try and sit as tall as you possibly can - Remember that sitting position is 90% reliant on the person to do it right, not the seat.

EXERCISE 7 A Chairless Day

Imagine that there are no chairs in the house. How can you function? Often times the results of this little experiment are predictable. We will engage our imagination and adapt. You can use a swiss ball instead of a chair for meal times. You can sit cross legged on the floor to work on the laptop. You can deep squat or kneel in front of the desk to work on desktop computer. You can have a lie down to watch telly or to read a book. It's not difficult. Just use your imagination and go a whole day without setting your rump on a chair. on a chair.

In the kitchen

Anatomical Neutral

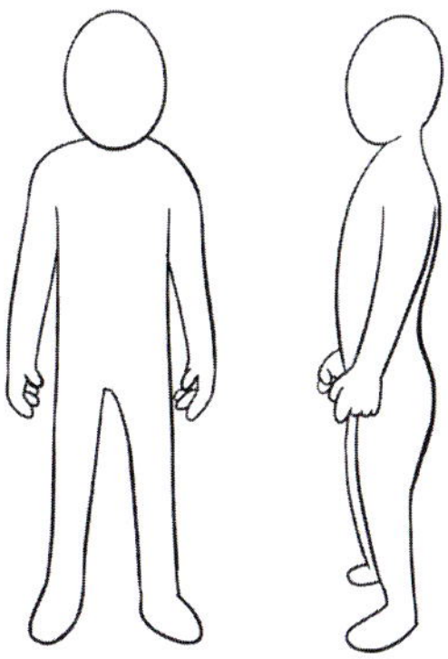

Most of the activities in the kitchen involve standing up. Therefore I urge you to re visit the chapter on anatomical neutral as needed to ensure best possible start to this chapter.

At all standing up jobs, be it chopping, cooking, washing up, or drying dishes we must maintain the active core that is achieved in the anatomical neutral. With active core and appropriate body positioning the arm movements become much easier for the brain to compute and for your body to tolerate without fatigue and strain. Those activities requiring movement, such as reaching into the cupboards, bending into the oven and the dishwasher must also begin from the neutral position.

Stoop

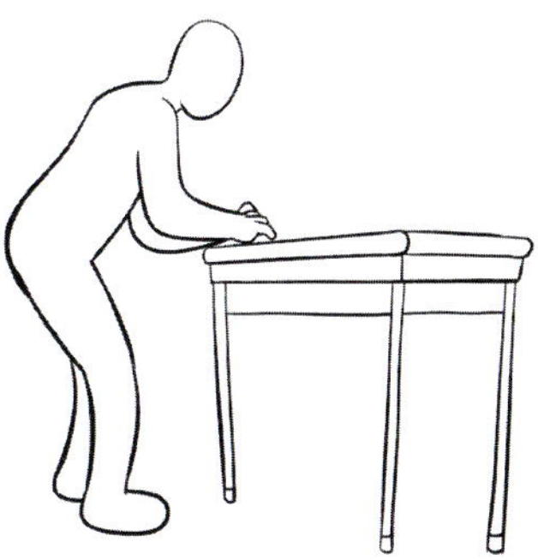

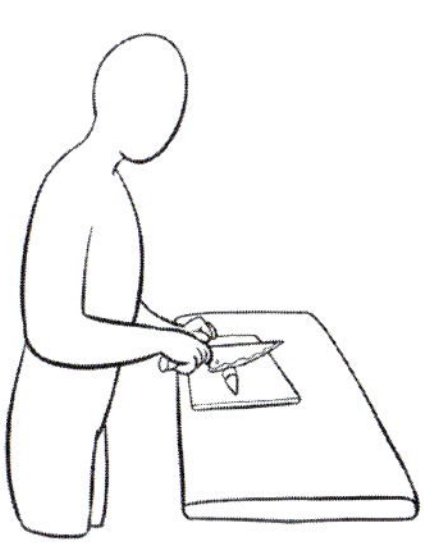

The key in terms of the kitchen work is the ability to get up or down to the correct height. i.e. if you need to bend down to reach the kitchen worktop comfortably or if you need to reach forward over the sink when washing up, you must learn to stoop. Stooping is different from bending. At least in the popular context. Most people who bend, do so from the spine leaving the low back vulnerable and exposed, with locked legs underneath to maximise the strain on the low back muscles and discs.

High Kneeling

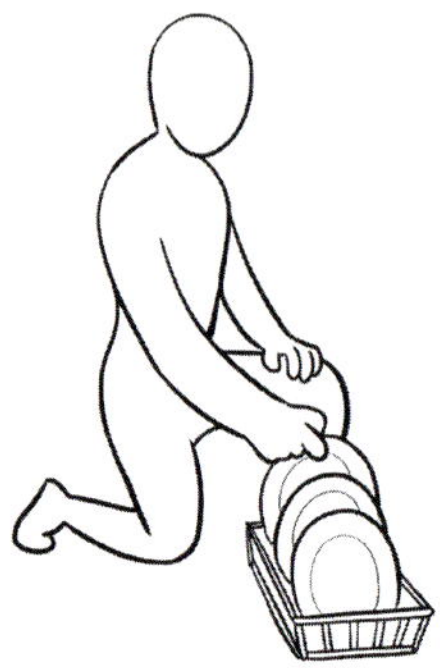

Four Point Kneeling

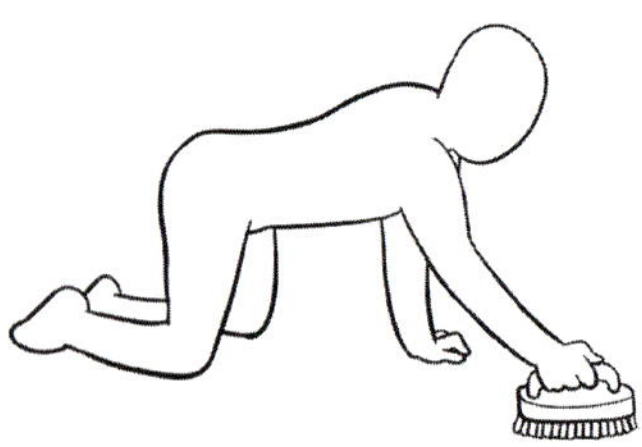

Instead stooping involves bending at the hip joints and maintaining good spinal alignment and core activation. Getting down a bit lower is easily achieved with a slight flex of the knees and the hips. Much in the same way as an elevator would move. The trunk simply goes up and down without spinal flexion.

The utilisation of the joints of the legs (hips, knees, and ankles) makes a lot of sense, because that is the reason we have these joints. They are designed for this kind of movement, even in sustained positions. Your back is badly designed for prolonged flexion due to the long lever arm of the upper body. The muscles of the low back become quickly fatigued and furthermore progressively lose their functional ability as a result. This process may lead to soreness, stiffness, pain and outright injury if repeated often enough.

When loading and unloading the dishwasher the utilisation of the legs is paramount when just putting a few bits in. A good strategy for unloading would be to divide the job into two distinct parts. First to utilise the high kneeling position to get close to the action and simply empty the contents onto the closest work surface. The second part, which you can do it standing and moving positions is to place the items into cupboards and drawers. You will avoid the temptation of bending incorrectly.

EXERCISE 8 Up and Down

- *Learn to get up and down without bending your spine. You really need to utilise your legs, including the hips, knees, ankles and the feet to achieve this. You may notice tightness in the hamstring (back of thigh) or the calf muscles as you first try it, but that will soon start to disperse as you practise. In order to get all the way down to a deep squat position, please hold onto a bannister, kitchen counter or similar to stop yourself falling over backwards. Remember, the further down you go, the more your bottom must stick out.*

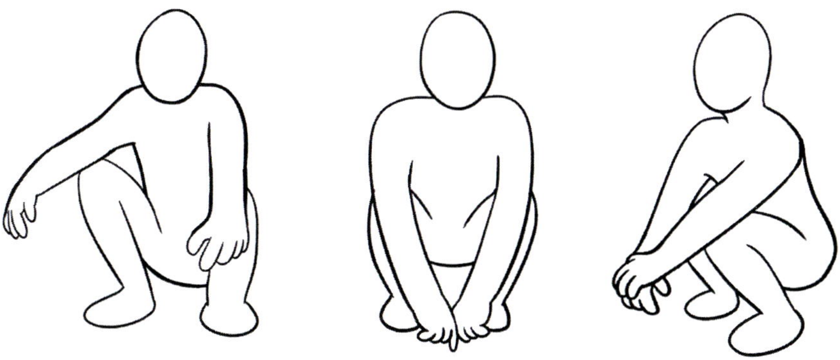

Cleaning

Scrubbing and polishing, as well as hoovering and dusting (and all manner of other cleaning related procedures and activities) are very repetitive by nature. This poses a possible problem due to the combination of poor technique and mounting fatigue. Again, please refer to the appropriate previous chapters as required.

One of the most hazardous activities in the home is hoovering. Surprising, isn't it? Nothing else really combines the worst possible posture (flexed and rotated spine, straight legs, and deactivated core muscles) and repetitive jerky movements of the upper limb, with a distasteful attitude leading to impatience and even violence in the execution of the task. Let's face it, as nobody really enjoys hoovering and we all would rather be doing something else it can become a volatile combination. Yet with a few little tweaks we can not only make it a safe activity, but actually a part of your home based workout routine. Getting a bit stronger, fitter, and more coordinated while hoovering - surely that would make it easier to tolerate.

EXERCISE 9 Tai Chi Hoovering

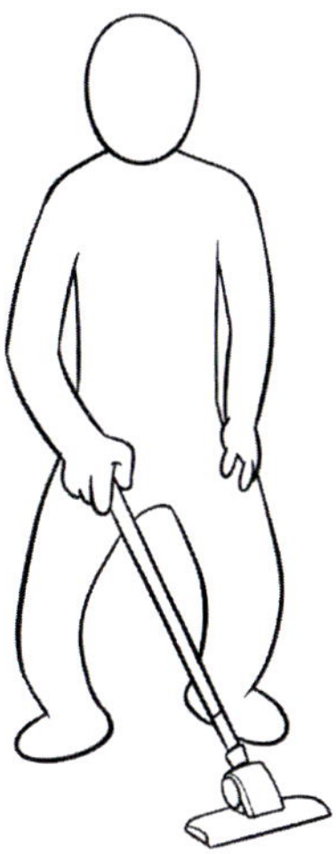

To make the most of hoovering we will utilise the modified Martial Arts stance. Start in the anatomical neutral position again. Holding the hoover in one hand. Split your stance wide and flex the legs to get the head of the hoover down to floor. Simply move the hoover across the floor by shifting your weight from one foot to the other and using your arms to push out for the extra bit of reach. You will notice that in this position your spinal angle remains perfect and your core muscles will activate virtually by themselves. Also you will notice how much harder your legs are working. For added difficulty you can squat a bit deeper.

When dusting and reaching up to shelves etc. remember to position your body in a way that requires the least compromise to your anatomical neutral position. Using a step or a little step ladder is a good idea. If you have trouble with balance and/or confidence then best to practice getting up and down the step or the ladder in a safe place, for example you can position the step next to a bannister or into a corner of the room where you have two walls to support yourself against.

When working low down, as in skirting board level, the deep squat position can be your greatest ally. It will be great for the mobilisation and strengthening of the legs and the low back.

If scrubbing the floor, please assume the correct "on all fours" position and resist the urge to reach too far. It is much better to move often and to reach less, simply to reduce the length of the lever arm. This will teach you better control through the shoulders and strengthen the midsection.

Awareness is again very important. Please take the crucial second before throwing yourself into it, as a quick think of how to do these things can be the difference between potion and poison. For example, hoovering the stairs. I know, professional cleaners work top to bottom, but in terms of reducing the excessive strain it may be better to hoover bottom to top. You can always remain in the anatomical neutral, instead of bending and twisting your spine to reach down the steps.

When moving heavy furniture it is of course advisable to enlist the help of another person where possible. A fully laden chest of drawers can easily weigh more than 100Kg. If lifting becomes too arduous, use rollers or sliders to help you if you need to drag furniture along the floor (you don't want to scratch the floor either). Simple rollers, such as a skateboard, or a slider (like a piece of cloth) can be placed under the feet of the piece of furniture making the object easier to push or drag. Again remember to hunker down enough to get your legs into the correct position, instead of bending your spine to get low enough.

In the Garden

The garden poses another kind of potential for injury. Not really due to the activities being inherently more challenging or risky, but the likelihood of one getting carried away and working for many hours without a break are much greater in the garden.

The two things to keep in mind in the garden therefore are pacing and positioning. The positioning is relatively straight forward, since the same principles apply outdoors and indoors. In terms of pacing one must remember to mix it up at regular intervals. Usually there is more than one job to be done in the garden at any given time. Why not simply work on each of these tasks for 30-40 minutes at a time and then move on to the next job with a little shake up in between? You can utilise an egg timer (or other sufficiently loud and obnoxious timed noise) to remind yourself to swap to another task.

It's also a good idea to mix up the lower body oriented and upper body oriented activities after one another, as well as sustained position activities with those that require more vigorous movement. Thus the body and brain will avoid stagnation and too much repetition, reducing the likelihood of fatigue and injury. A bit of planning does go a long way.

Probably the single most problematic activity in the garden is weeding. Most people complain of sore back and shoulders after a long bout of kneeling in the flower beds. It makes perfect sense as often times the body position is far from optimal. Many people choose to stay rooted to one spot and try to reach as far as possible before moving. If the flower bed is too wide or long the reach becomes too much for the body to handle, especially if the attention wanders from good core muscle activation. It would be much more sensible to move along more frequently, and maybe even switch from one side of the flower bed to the other. The correct four point kneeling position is important, yet mixing it up by using the deep squat position instead of the perpetual "kneel and reach" would provide great variety.

When digging, mowing the lawn, pruning or trimming the hedges, the body positioning again is paramount. When any kind of an external load is applied to the human body, and furthermore this external load is being swung and moved around, adequate stabilisation is not only advisable but a necessity. Remember, your lumbar discs are the most vulnerable when the bent spine and rotation movements are combined. Bracing the abdominal muscles is much more effective when the trunk is in good alignment and the legs are utilised correctly.

EXERCISE 10 Remember to Brace

- *When picking up a garden tool, such as the lawn mower, the strimmer, the hedge trimmer, the power washer, or even the spade for that matter, stop for a second and take a moment to engage your abdominal muscles. When you consciously switch these muscles on they will cause the rest of your core to activate, at the same time producing a protective corset like effect around your midsection. Start moving slowly to begin with and trying to maintain the muscular activation, only speed up once you feel confident to do so. Stop from time to time to switch the muscles back on again in case your attention has wandered.*

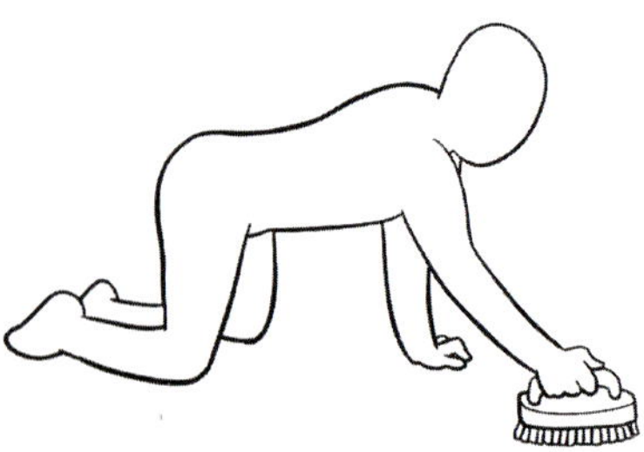

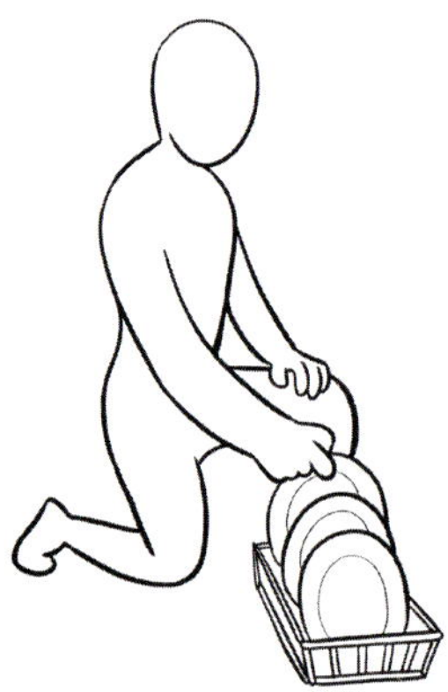

In the Bathroom

Stoop

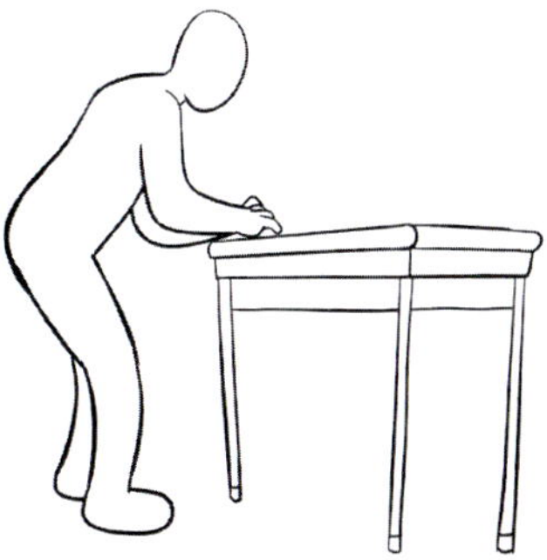

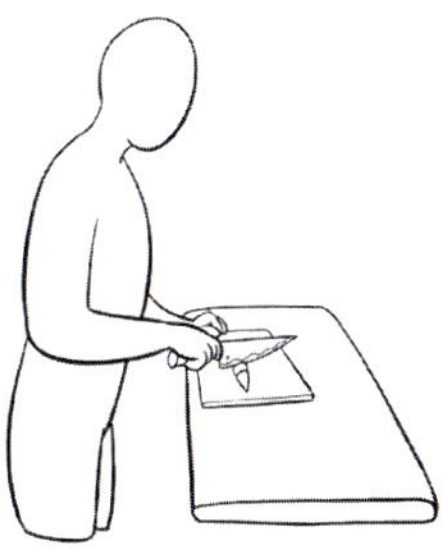

Another important daily activity is on the hygiene front. We all shower or bathe, we clean our teeth, shave, apply make-up, and use the toilet. Now, you may think I have gone off my rocker bringing this stuff up, but trust me, it's important to cover a few bases.

To shower or to bathe? There is one potential danger in the bathtub when it comes to your back. I never recommend a hot relaxing bath when you have acute pain in the back. The reason is that the muscles will be holding you tightly for a reason. They are trying to protect you from further damage, much in the same way as support structures are used to prop up a wobbly house. The bath tends to cause too much relaxation in the muscles and due to the slouchy positioning in the bath, the back can slip out even worse. In acute pain situation the shower is much better as you can let the hot water massage those tight muscles, with your back in a neutral position, and getting out of the shower is much less problematic.

When not in acute pain, a bath is absolutely fine. A good helping of Epsom salts will also work wonders in drawing out a lot of the toxins and metabolites from the system and leave you feeling very relaxed.

The problems with the activities at the sink and the mirror are caused by the bending of the spine. The all too popular choice of locked back knees and curved back when cleaning teeth or washing face is a rather poor one, as it places all the load on the long muscles of the low back, instead of the legs.

The better option is to use a modified martial arts stance, with feet a bit wider than hip width, and the height adjustment taking place with the flexion of hips, knees and ankles. The back should stay very neutral in this position. This will not only spare your back from the unnecessary strain in a bad position, but also gives your thighs and buttocks a bit of a work out. The other option is the stooping movement, which is best applied in short term activities such as getting down to rinse your mouth or to wash your face.

EXERCISE 11 Brain Training 101

To stimulate your brain more, you can do this simple drill. Use your non-dominant hand to clean your teeth. Yes, that's correct. A right handed person should use the left hand for certain precision tasks each day to stimulate the motor cortex and the non-dominant hemisphere of the brain further. This can have a good effect on your movement skills in general. Shaving and applying make-up should only be undertaken with the non-dominant hand once a certain level of dexterity and confidence has been reached. To further enhance the brain stimulating effect, please stand on one leg while cleaning your teeth with the non-dominant hand. Feel free to swap sides from time to time. Now a simple everyday task becomes a whole lot more interesting and truly a source of learning.

When you have back pain going to the toilet can be very painful. Simply lowering yourself down and getting back up again can be torturous, let alone having to fight through a bout of constipation to get the job done. When in pain, it is good to try and facilitate a good bowel movement by all natural means, such as plenty of fibre in the diet and adequate hydration, as well as good positioning on the loo. Also when taking certain painkillers, such as co-codamol (codeine) it is a good idea to take a Senna tablet along with it to reduce likelihood of constipation.

When on the toilet, take your time. Don't try and force it by pushing very hard. This may have dire consequences in terms of your rectal health, and there is even evidence of strokes brought on by forceful pushing on the loo. A simple aid to a better toilet experience is to use a step under the feet to simulate a near squatting position. There are now various products available on the market designed for this specific purpose, yet a simple children's step is usually adequate. The squatting position helps to straighten out the bottom part of the colon and the rectum and it can also help you maintain a better spinal angle. If you are suffering with constipation, however, it is very important to know why. Often times the causes are in the diet and they can be relatively easy to spot but can take a while to sort out.

Additional Tips

There is a whole world out there of helpful tips and pointers for helping you to live your life more fully each day. I only really wish to touch on a couple of topics here as they will be discussed more fully in my upcoming works.

Exercise is a big topic and a tough one at that. It seems to be a bit of a marmite of life. Some people love it and can't get enough of it, yet others struggle to find any enjoyment in it. Everyone knows that exercise is important. Everyone knows that by exercising regularly you can improve your health and reduce likelihood of disease and early death. Everyone knows that exercising on a daily basis can make you feel better. Yet, somehow the threshold is too high. Here is the rub. People go to the gym or start running because they feel that it's what they are supposed to do. However, why don't we all take a step back and see what it is that we would like to do? What would be fun? Preposterous, right? Surely exercise is not supposed to be fun? But come on now. You have the right to choose to do anything that is preferential to grunting and sweating in the gym. Use your imagination and choose an activity or sport that appeals to you.

So how to get started and how to keep going after the initial excitement has started to wane? The first thing you need is a motivator. Something that is big enough to make you question your own abilities and at the same time fill you with a sense of awe. Something that would make you feel like "a million bucks" if you were to achieve it. We all have had those dreams that we never acted on due to a variety of excuses... No more excuses - get on with it. Secondly you need a plan. It's much more difficult to slip out of something when it's written down and you are committed to it. Hire a coach. Pay the money - trust me, it will make you commit much more than simply winging it from day to day. It will be money well spent.

Summary

Today is the first day of the rest of your life. As you get up in the morning, you are faced with a choice. A choice by which you can choose whether you will be more or less than you were yesterday. There is no middle ground. There is no playing for keeps. You will either choose to expand, grow and learn, or you will choose to fade away a bit more. The choice is yours to make. With this freedom to choose comes responsibility for your own actions, and the fear of the responsibility is what will reduce many people and cause them to shy away from living their dreams. But not you.

The tips in this book will help you get started on your journey of creating a more resilient body. They are intended as a guide to be learned and applied to your daily activities and thus reducing the unwanted injury potential that constantly distracts you from your greater abilities. The brain and the body are magnificent creations, designed to work in harmony and cooperation in order to help you live the life of your dreams. A life, where pain is transient and it is dealt with appropriate conscious actions, rather than a life of strife, suffering and fear of your own self.

No more excuses.

Get out there and live!

The Last Words

Thank you for reading through this book. I hope that you have found it helpful. The advice in this book has been rigorously tested on the field by thousands of patients over the years, and I have no doubt that it can provide you with a helpful hint or two, and hopefully open your eyes to seeing the home in a different light. In a way this book contains the basic skills of survival in the home environment, at least when it comes to your back health. With awareness and regular practice these skills will soon become automatic and unconscious habits. With the elimination of a whole bunch of irritants from your life, such as bad posture, I am certain you will enjoy greater spinal health and less pain.

I would like to draw your attention back to the challenge set earlier on in the book, remember the challenge to make your dreams a reality. Had you forgotten already? In a way our lives revolve around controlling the controllables, and with better grasp on your health and as you experience less pain and better enjoyment of every aspect of your life reaching for those dreams will become more and more realistic. Why not? Why shouldn't you? Who's stopping you?

You can check out my website, **www.resilientthree.com** *(to be launched in 2017)* for books on various health and lifestyle related topics. I will also be making most of the material available in video format in due course.

You can follow us on **Twitter (@R3silient)** for more updates and news.

Yours in health,

Mika Janhunen D.C., M(Chiro), ICCSP, MRCC
DIRECTOR

Shepperton Chiropractic Clinic Ltd,
Resilient Three (Body, Mind and Spirit) – Wellness Coaching

Notes

Notes

Notes

FICHE DE

DOCUMENT RÉDIGÉ
MAITRE EN
(UNIVERSITÉ LIBRE DE BRUXELLES)

Pensées

Blaise Pascal

lePetitLittéraire.fr

Blaise Pascal
Scientifique, moraliste, philosophe et théologien français

- **Né en 1623 à Clairmont**
- **Décédé en 1662 à Paris**
- **Quelques-unes de ses œuvres :**
  Les Provinciales (1656-1657), correspondance
  L'Art de persuader (1660), œuvre philosophique
  Pensées (1670), ensemble de fragments

Blaise Pascal (1623-1662) est un homme de lettres, un scientifique et un théologien. Dès son plus jeune âge, il se distingue par une intelligence hors normes. Adolescent, il compose un traité des sons, puis un essai sur les coniques et, à l'âge de dix-neuf ans, il invente la machine à calculer. En 1654, Pascal est victime d'un accident de carrosse qui lui fait prendre conscience de la fragilité de la vie. L'incident marque le début de ses préoccupations religieuses. Son idéal chrétien le fait renoncer aux sciences : il se consacre à la réflexion philosophique et religieuse, et rédige *Les Provinciales*, dix-huit lettres de défense des thèses jansénistes.

Blaise Pascal influence grandement la méthode scientifique, les théories économiques et les sciences sociales. Il décède de maladie sans avoir vu publier les *Pensées*.

Pensées
L'œuvre d'un moraliste et d'un théologien

- **Genre :** essai
- **Édition de référence :** *Pensées*, Paris, Éditions France Loisirs, coll. « Les grands écrivains choisis par l'Académie Goncourt », 1986.
- **1re édition :** 1670
- **Thématiques :** christianisme, bonheur, politique, humanité, justice

Œuvre posthume de Pascal publiée en 1670, les *Pensées* répondent à une volonté de démontrer que l'homme ne peut trouver la paix intérieure et le bonheur véritable qu'en acceptant d'être touché par la grâce de Dieu. L'homme sans Dieu est misérable et fini alors que Dieu est toute-puissance et infini.

La politique, l'homme et le souverain bien sont les grands thèmes abordés dans l'œuvre par le philosophe théologien. Les échos pascaliens dans la modernité sont nombreux et l'actualité de ses réflexions permanente.

RÉSUMÉ

SECTION 1 – PENSÉES SUR L'ESPRIT ET SUR LE STYLE

Dans l'esprit de géométrie, les principes sont des principes connus sur lesquels on ne peut que bien raisonner. Dans l'esprit de finesse, les principes ne se laissent pas manier aisément et on les sent plus qu'on ne les voit. Il est difficile de les faire sentir à ceux qui ne les sentent pas d'eux-mêmes. Leur objet ne s'appréhende pas selon un raisonnement progressif, mais seulement dans leur totalité. L'esprit de finesse relève des choses en rapport avec les sentiments, l'esprit de géométrie des choses de raisonnement.

SECTION 2 – MISÈRE DE L'HOMME SANS DIEU

Les hommes ont voulu comprendre les principes des choses jusqu'à connaitre le tout avec un infini orgueil, mais un homme n'est rien dans l'infini et ne peut comprendre les principes des choses en totalité. Il se situe entre le néant et le tout, et doit reconnaitre sa portée limitée. Le néant et le tout ne se retrouvent qu'en Dieu, toute-puissance et siège de la réalité de toute chose :

> « Les impressions anciennes, les charmes de la nouveauté, les apparences, les sentiments et notre propre intérêt sont des causes de jugements mauvais. Tout ceci domine

> la raison jusqu'à disposer de tout : la justice, le bonheur et le tout du monde. L'homme n'est donc que déguisement, que mensonge et hypocrisie, et en soi-même et à l'égard des autres. Il ne veut pas qu'on lui dise la vérité, il évite de la dire aux autres ; et toutes ces dispositions, si éloignées de la justice et de la raison, ont une racine naturelle dans son cœur. (p. 59)

La condition humaine se compose d'inconstance, d'inquiétude et d'ennui. C'est une condition malheureuse à laquelle l'homme tente vainement d'échapper à travers le divertissement (le jeu, la guerre, les femmes, etc.). La mort, la misère et l'ignorance sont ignorées puisqu'inguérissables et rendant malheureux. Le divertissement est la seule chose qui nous console de nos misères.

SECTION 3 – DE LA NÉCESSITÉ DU PARI

Dieu met la religion dans l'esprit par les raisons et dans le cœur par la grâce. Il est infiniment incompréhensible puisqu'il n'a aucun rapport avec nous, êtres limités. Nous sommes incapables de savoir si il est ni ce qu'il est parce qu'un chaos infini nous sépare.

Nous ne pouvons connaitre Dieu que par la soumission de la raison. La foi est affaire de cœur et non de science. Elle est nécessaire et permet de s'éloigner des plaisirs empestés pour embrasser l'honnêteté, la fidélité, l'humilité et la sincérité.

SECTION 4 – DES MOYENS DE CROIRE

Il faut se soumettre ostensiblement à Dieu et l'attendre à l'extérieur pour qu'il nous visite à l'intérieur. Il soumet notre âme naturellement sans art et sans argument. Tout le raisonnement se réduit à céder au sentiment ; puisque la religion est mystérieuse et surnaturelle, elle ne peut se soumettre à la raison. L'impossibilité de prouver l'existence de Dieu par la raison ne prouve rien d'autre que la faiblesse de notre raison. Les premiers principes se sentent et viennent du cœur ; les hommes qui ont la disposition de la religion dans le cœur n'ont pas besoin de plus pour comprendre qu'il faut aimer Dieu et ne haïr que soi-même. Dieu incline lui-même à croire, il n'en faut pas davantage pour être persuadé.

SECTION 5 –
LA JUSTICE ET LES RAISONS DES EFFETS

La justice devrait être la même pour tous les États du monde et dans tous les temps puisqu'elle n'est pas dans les coutumes, mais dans les lois naturelles. Or tout branle avec le temps, et selon le bon vouloir des rois et des dictateurs. Les puissances s'établissent selon les fantaisies du moment ; c'est pourquoi, il n'y a pas de constance dans la loi et la justice. Aussi le peuple prend-il l'antiquité des coutumes comme une preuve de leur vérité, ce qui explique la fausseté de ses opinions. Les actions de l'homme sont gouvernées par la faiblesse, la concupiscence et les rapports de force.

SECTION 6 – LES PHILOSOPHES

La pensée est grande par sa nature, mais basse par ses défauts : la pensée est aisément manipulable, on peut prouver toujours tout et son contraire. L'homme sans Dieu est donc dans l'ignorance de tout et dans un inévitable malheur car il ne peut s'assurer d'aucune vérité alors qu'il le voudrait.

L'homme doit connaitre sa bassesse tout autant que sa grandeur et jamais l'un sans l'autre. La recherche du vrai bien est inutile, il faut juste tendre les bras au libérateur.

SECTION 7 – LA MORALE ET LA DOCTRINE

Dieu est le véritable bien. Il a voulu se rendre parfaitement connaissable à ceux qui le cherchent sincèrement et caché de ceux qui le fuient cordialement.

La vraie nature de l'homme, son vrai bien, la vraie vertu et la vraie religion ne peuvent être connus séparément. Dieu seul donne la sagesse.

La religion nous apprend que par un homme (le péché originel), la liaison entre l'homme et Dieu a été rompue, puis qu'elle a été rétablie par le Christ : ce dernier est le médiateur rendant possible la communication avec Dieu. Les prophéties sont des preuves solides de l'existence de Jésus-Christ.

L'écriture, le péché originel et le Christ prouvent absolument Dieu, la doctrine et la morale. Le Christ nous fait connaitre notre misère puisqu'il est le réparateur de notre misère. Or on ne connait bien Dieu qu'en connaissant nos iniquités. Par conséquent, sans l'écriture qui n'a que Jésus pour objet, nous ne connaissons rien, pas même nous-mêmes.

SECTION 8 – LES FONDEMENTS DE LA RELIGION CHRÉTIENNE

Il faut connaitre Dieu et sa misère, et non l'un sans l'autre. Les hommes sont à la fois indignes de Dieu par leur corruption et capables de Dieu par leur première nature. Nous sommes misérables et séparés de Dieu, mais rachetés par Jésus-Christ. La vérité de la religion se reconnait dans l'obscurité même de la religion. Dieu est caché en partie et découvert en partie, et cela est utile : l'obscurité pour que l'homme sente sa corruption et la lumière pour qu'il puisse espérer un remède.

ÉCLAIRAGES

NAISSANCE DE LA FOI

Dans la famille de Pascal, tout le monde est croyant, d'une foi sincère mais tiède. Ce n'est qu'en 1646 que Pascal vit « sa première conversion » lorsque les frères Deschamps, appelés au chevet de son père pour sa jambe démise, transmettent à la famille l'idéologie augustinienne. Sa sœur Jacqueline entre alors en 1652 à la communauté religieuse de Port-Royal, qui applique la pensée de saint Augustin dans sa version la plus sévère et intransigeante : les clercs, théologiens, savants et laïcs que le couvent abrite mènent une vie extrêmement simple et austère.

La « seconde conversion » de Pascal survient une nuit de 1654 après un coma dû à un accident de calèche. À son réveil, le savant décrit une expérience mystique. Pascal clame avec passion sa foi nouvelle et se consacre définitivement à la religion. Il se rend quelque temps à Port-Royal dont il embrasse la cause bien qu'il n'ait jamais officiellement été membre de la communauté. C'est à cette époque qu'il commence à travailler à son grand projet d'*Apologie de la religion chrétienne*.

NAISSANCE D'UNE ŒUVRE

Pascal n'a jamais écrit un livre s'intitulant *Pensées*. Ce sont les éditeurs qui ont présenté les brouillons épars que l'auteur a laissés sous la forme d'une œuvre plète qui est en grande partie constituée des documents préparatoires à la rédaction de l'*Apologie de la religion chrétienne* : cette œuvre nouvelle construite sur les ruines de l'*Apologie* est autant de leur main que de celle de Pascal. D'après les éditeurs, le théologien annonçait lui-même une volonté de présentation délibérément discontinue sous la forme d'un recueil de maximes (unités segmentées). Cependant, il n'est pas exclu que cette annonce soit en réalité celle des éditeurs.

Pascal a hâtivement griffonné ses idées sur des feuillets pour échapper à la fugacité de ses pensées en les figeant. Les *Pensées* témoignent donc d'une écriture de l'urgence, symptôme du drame humain qu'est l'horrible écoulement du temps et des choses. Ce recours au « bloc-notes » explique le caractère télégraphique de l'œuvre. Ce n'est encore qu'une esquisse, une promesse de discours.

Les proches de l'écrivain ont découvert à sa mort des dossiers emplis de feuillets et cousus par un fil. Des thèmes ont pu en être dégagés sans pour autant qu'on puisse conclure aux parties effectives d'un plan envisagé. Peut-être n'était-ce là qu'une méthode de classement personnel. L'entourage de Pascal a d'abord décidé de recopier les liasses à l'identique, mais, en un siècle où l'on n'avait que dédain pour les formes décousues, le texte était impubliable tel quel. En 1670, la décision d'une édition sélective et corrigée a donc été prise : l'édition de Port-Royal, une version trop épurée qui escamote la syntaxe si personnelle de l'écrivain, son audace, de même que certains passages clés de son argumentation. Au XIXe siècle, une édition enfin intégrale des *Pensées* a été réclamée. Néanmoins, bien qu'exhaustives, les éditions modernes restent des interprétations personnelles des éditeurs sur la reconstitution de l'ordre des fragments. Les *Pensées* sont une œuvre incertaine, mouvante et malléable qui ne peut plus être que coulée dans le moule de ses interprètes.

L'AUGUSTINISME

L'influence de saint Augustin (philosophe et théologien chrétien né en 354 et mort en 430) sur l'œuvre pascalienne est grande. Pascal reprend de l'évêque une partie conséquente de sa conception noire et tragique de la religion. Il partage l'idée que le péché originel est la racine de la corruption irréversible du genre humain. L'homme est un pantin manipulé par trois sortes de concupiscence : la curiosité, l'orgueil et la luxure. Face à ces tentations, la morale augustinienne préconise le seul souci de Dieu contre les vanités de la science, une humilité profonde contre l'aspiration au pouvoir et l'abstinence absolue comme remède aux tentations de la chair. La vraie certitude se trouve dans la foi et non dans la raison. Pascal ne dit pas autre chose. Il défend un christianisme coulé dans la terreur et la restriction qui n'assure le salut qu'à très peu d'individus, élus d'une loterie par la grâce divine. La prédestination de l'homme est tragique ; en effet, peu importe ses actes, il ne maitrise pas son devenir.

CLÉS DE LECTURE

UNE ŒUVRE THÉOLOGIQUE

Les *Pensées* témoignent du système des croyances du XVIIe siècle. La religion exerce à l'époque une emprise énorme sur les esprits : elle impose partout ses lois et oriente la pensée. Les autorités ecclésiastiques contrôlent les œuvres publiées et régissent la censure, et on brule les hérétiques au nom de la pensée unique. C'est un christianisme nettement plus sombre que celui d'aujourd'hui où la peur de Dieu est centrale. Par conséquent, une lecture rigoureusement historique des *Pensées* est de mise : le lecteur doit éviter l'écueil des anachronismes pour ne pas être heurté par les propos de Pascal et ne pas passer à côté de la grandeur de l'œuvre.

La figure de Dieu

Pascal retient des Écritures le Dieu grand, puissant et terrible. C'est un être universel capable de vous perdre à tout instant. Il est à la fois menace du châtiment et consolation. Autrement dit, Dieu est autant douceur, amour et charité que vengeance et terreur. Il est caché aux yeux de la raison ou de l'âme, mais pas entièrement : il se laisse entrevoir sans paraitre tout à fait. Cette dissimulation partielle de Dieu trie les hommes entre ceux de l'élite et ceux de la masse aveugle. Ceux qui le cherchent en toute sincérité le trouvent, mais il reste caché à ceux qui ne le cherchent pas. Désirer Dieu, c'est donc déjà le posséder.

Le péché originel

Pascal livre une vision tragique du christianisme selon laquelle l'homme est irrémédiablement malheureux parce qu'il sait qu'il a été heureux et qu'il ne l'est plus. La chute impose à l'humanité souffrance et pénitence, et les chrétiens doivent payer indéfiniment pour un crime qu'ils n'ont pas commis en fonction d'une justice divine dont le principe échappe à la raison. La condition humaine est misérable puisque l'homme vit avec le souvenir du bonheur perdu ; c'est là le plus cruel des tourments. La première nature de l'homme est irrévocablement perdue et le manque de bonheur impossible à combler. L'œuvre est marquée d'un sentiment d'angoisse et d'étroitesse lié à la condition mortelle de l'homme, ce qui rapproche les *Pensées* du genre tragique.

Le Christ

Pascal réduit la doctrine chrétienne à deux puissances égales et opposées : la corruption de la nature et la rédemption de Jésus-Christ. Le Christ unit en lui la nature humaine et la nature divine pour réconcilier les hommes avec Dieu en sa nature divine. Il incarne la rédemption. Par là, le Christ dispense un double enseignement : il y a un Dieu dont les hommes sont méritants et un Dieu dont les hommes sont indignes à cause de la corruption de la nature. Réparateur, rédempteur et libérateur, Jésus répare la faute originelle et ouvre l'accès au salut. Le Christ est également un intermédiaire. La communication entre le fini et l'infini est impossible sans médiateur ; c'est lui qui rend possible la réunification entre Dieu et les hommes. Le Christ tient une place absolument centrale : sans lui, nous ne connaitrions ni la vie, ni la mort, ni Dieu, ni nous-mêmes.

La nécessité de la foi

Pascal ne cherche pas à transmettre la foi puisqu'elle est intransmissible par le raisonnement, mais à prouver sa nécessité. La foi est un don de Dieu. Elle dépasse et contredit la raison. La croyance, c'est l'abandon de la raison au profit d'une vérité supérieure qui la heurte parfois. Mais si Pascal n'essaie pas de transmettre la foi, il recommande néanmoins une morale et un mode de vie conformes à la vie d'un chrétien. Même l'homme qui n'est pas visité par la grâce de Dieu peut se préparer intérieurement à devenir chrétien en vivant extérieurement comme tel. Dieu pourrait dans ce cas octroyer sa grâce *in fine*. Cependant, en augustinien, le penseur affirme que tous les hommes ne seront pas sauvés.

GRANDEUR ET MISÈRE DE L'HOMME

L'argument essentiel de l'œuvre est celui des contrariétés, à savoir des contradictions internes de l'homme : celui-ci est à la fois plein de grandeur et plein de misère. Pascal considère le christianisme comme le seul système philosophique qui exprime globalement ces deux aspects contradictoires, c'est la doctrine qui rend compte de tout. Avant la chute, l'homme était proche de Dieu et rendu digne par lui qui le plaçait au centre de la création. C'est le souvenir de cette félicité à jamais perdue qui fait la grandeur de l'homme. Sa misère a quant à elle pour origine le péché originel qui condamne l'homme à des tourments permanents.

La conciliation des contrariétés

La vérité complète est faite de l'union de deux contraires : l'homme est à la fois grandeur et misère. Pascal remet en cause le principe de non-contradiction qui stipule qu'une proposition donnée ne peut être à la fois vraie et fausse. L'erreur est dans l'incomplétude et non dans la fausseté d'une des deux propositions. Pascal dénonce le stoïcisme d'Épictète qui ne voit que la grandeur de l'homme et le scepticisme de Montaigne qui n'en voit que sa misère : « C'est donc de ces lumières imparfaites qu'il arrive que l'un, connaissant les devoirs de l'homme et ignorant son impuissance, se perd dans la présomption, et que l'autre, connaissant l'impuissance et non le devoir, s'abat dans la lâcheté. » (extrait de l'*Entretien avec M. de Sacy*, 1655) Le christianisme dépasse les philosophies en unifiant des thèses opposées. Les vérités incompatibles dans les doctrines humaines s'accordent grâce à la vérité de l'Évangile. Plus encore, l'homme n'est pas au milieu, mais simultanément très haut et très bas. La morale chrétienne est une correction permanente qui abaisse les hommes orgueilleux et élève les hommes humiliés.

La pensée

C'est par la pensée que l'homme se hisse au-dessus du règne animal. La pensée fait la grandeur de l'homme. L'homme est à la fois corps et esprit, mais l'esprit dépasse infiniment le corps. Il y a un contraste absolu entre la faiblesse du corps et la puissance de l'esprit. Ontologiquement, l'esprit est supérieur à l'intégralité de l'univers matériel : l'esprit se révèle infiniment plus vaste que le tout de l'univers. C'est en cela que l'homme est à la fois profondément insignifiant et suprêmement digne. Mais si la pensée signale la grandeur de l'homme, elle est aussi le drame essentiel qui rend possible la prise de conscience de l'ampleur de sa détresse. L'homme est misérable, mais grand d'en avoir conscience. La principale marque de grandeur, la pensée, est donc encore la misère.

Le divertissement

Le divertissement est la réponse médiocre à la volonté d'échapper à la misère et il confirme la condition malheureuse de l'homme puisque si l'homme était heureux, il n'aurait pas besoin de se détourner de sa pensée par le divertissement. Sans divertissement, l'homme sombre dans l'ennui, puis dans le désespoir absolu. Cette solution ridicule ne fait que masquer le problème sans jamais le résoudre et, le plus souvent, jette l'homme dans l'indignité. Le jeu et les plaisirs corporels sont indignes de la grandeur de sa pensée. De plus, il est foncièrement inefficace puisqu'il n'a pas de but extrinsèque. Le divertissement pascalien est comparable au refoulement freudien. Tous deux sont des tentatives d'oubli de pensées douloureuses qui finissent forcément par un échec : les idées dérangeantes reviennent toujours, entrainant avec elles de nombreux tourments. Pascal veut dénoncer cette forme d'aveuglement qu'est le divertissement. Hors Dieu, il n'y a pas d'issue à l'angoisse de la vacuité. Une prolifération de faire ne compensera jamais la carence d'être.

Les puissances trompeuses et la concupiscence

Les puissances trompeuses constituent tout ce qui peut nous plonger dans l'erreur et sont un obstacle au vrai. Parmi elles, on distingue :

- l'imagination, l'irréductible part d'irrationalité que l'homme porte en lui, qui domine le sujet et suspend ses sens. À cause d'elle, l'homme ne maitrise plus sa propre vie intérieure. Pascal cherche à rendre à l'homme une vue plus saine du réel ;
- l'intérêt ou amour-propre ;
- la coutume. L'homme prend inconsciemment la convention locale pour l'universalité. Habitudes de pensée, idéologies et traditions sont les coutumes dont parle Pascal et qu'on nommerait aujourd'hui la culture, par opposition à la nature. Elle est à l'origine de la plupart de nos convictions et certitudes dont la majorité ne trouvent pas racine dans la raison. Les coutumes sont des preuves plus fortes pour la raison que l'expérience. Pascal fait le constat de l'extrême relativité des lois qui varient d'un endroit à l'autre et changent en fonction des époques : chacun suit les mœurs de son pays et de son temps. La constatation de ces vérités si friables impose la quête d'une vérité stable et universelle.

La concupiscence est quant à elle un obstacle moral qui se décline selon trois aspects : orgueil, curiosité et concupiscence de la chair.

La fugacité

Elle rejoint le grand thème philosophique et littéraire de la vanité de toute chose. Le propre de la condition humaine, conséquence de la chute, est l'éphémérité. Cette fugacité des choses s'oppose à l'immobilité et à l'éternité divines. L'homme n'est qu'inconstance et incohérence.

LE RAISONNEMENT

L'œuvre est une longue argumentation qui relève pleinement d'une rhétorique. Pascal sait utiliser les moyens adaptés pour persuader ses lecteurs. L'auteur accorde une grande importance à la disposition des mots et au plan, et revendique un style simple et naturel par opposition à l'éclat de l'éloquence. L'écrivain déploie plusieurs formes de raisonnement :

- le raisonnement inductif : raisonnement qui consiste à partir d'un cas particulier pour en déduire une loi générale. Exemple : « Qui voudra connaître à plein la vanité de l'homme n'a qu'à considérer les causes et les effets de l'amour. [...] Le nez de Cléopâtre, s'il eût été plus court, toute la face de la terre aurait changé. » (p. 82-83) Pascal déduit ici du charme individuel de Cléopâtre les bouleversements universels que peut causer l'amour ;

- le raisonnement analogique : raisonnement par association d'idées. De certains points communs visibles entre deux situations, on en conclut l'existence d'autres ressemblances moins manifestes. Exemple : « Qu'on ne dise pas que je n'ai rien dit de nouveau, la disposition des matières est nouvelle. Quand on joue à la paume, c'est une même balle dont on joue l'un et l'autre, mais l'un la place mieux » (p. 20) ;
- le raisonnement déductif : le raisonnement déductif part d'une idée générale, d'un principe, d'une loi pour en tirer une conséquence particulière. Pascal dit par exemple, à peu près, que les preuves dont la négation constitue un péché sont indubitables ; or, les contemporains du Christ qui contestaient les miracles étaient des pécheurs ; donc, les miracles constituent une preuve indubitable ;
- le raisonnement à fortiori : raisonnement par lequel on montre qu'une vérité en entraine une autre, étayée d'arguments plus puissants. Une loi qui se vérifie dans un premier cas à première vue peu favorable se vérifiera à plus forte raison dans d'autres cas plus favorables : « Si les choses naturelles surpassent [la raison], que dira-t-on des surnaturelles ? » (p. 127) ;
- le raisonnement par l'absurde : il s'agit de démontrer la validité d'une hypothèse donnée par l'absurdité à laquelle aboutit l'hypothèse inverse. Exemple : « Si notre condition était véritablement heureuse, il ne faudrait pas nous divertir d'y penser » ;

- le raisonnement mathématique : argumentation sous forme de preuve scientifique absolument et définitivement indiscutable. C'est un raisonnement qui se veut imparable : « Quand il y aurait une infinité de hasards dont un seul serait pour vous, vous auriez encore raison de gager un pour avoir deux [...] ; mais il y a ici une infinité de vie infiniment heureuse à gagner, un hasard de gain contre un nombre fini de hasards de perte, et ce que vous jouez est fini. »

PISTES DE RÉFLEXION

QUELQUES QUESTIONS POUR APPROFONDIR SA RÉFLEXION...

- Les professionnels du livre trouvent que l'œuvre pascalienne est un casse-tête à classer. Comment l'expliquez-vous ?
- Quel lien peut-on établir entre la théorie freudienne du refoulement et les réflexions de Pascal sur l'idée insoutenable de notre mort ?
- Jean Mesnard voit en Pascal un précurseur de l'existentialisme contemporain. Êtes-vous d'accord avec lui ?
- Quelle(s) différence(s) y a-t-il entre l'ennui pascalien et le sentiment de l'absurde chez Camus ?
- *Un roi sans divertissement* contient des citations de Pascal. La vision du monde de Jean Giono est-elle semblable à celle de Pascal ?
- Quelle est l'influence de saint Augustin sur les *Pensées* de Pascal ?
- Pascal se partage entre augustinisme et jansénisme. Expliquez.
- Relevez quelques apories (contradictions impossibles à résoudre) dans l'argumentation pascalienne.
- Quel rapport Pascal entretient-il avec le scepticisme (doctrine philosophique selon laquelle l'homme ne peut atteindre la connaissance de la vérité) ?

POUR ALLER PLUS LOIN

ÉDITION DE RÉFÉRENCE

- PASCAL B., *Pensées,* Éditions France Loisirs, coll. « Les grands écrivains choisis par l'Académie Goncourt », 1986.

ÉTUDE DE RÉFÉRENCE

- TOURRETTE É., Pensées. *Grandeur et misère de l'homme,* Paris, Éditions Bréal, coll. « Connaissance d'une œuvre », 2008.

SUR LEPETITLITTÉRAIRE.FR

- Commentaire des fragments 325 et 326 des *Pensées*
- Commentaire des fragments 301 à 337 des *Pensées*

Retrouvez notre offre complète sur lePetitLittéraire.fr

- des fiches de lectures
- des commentaires littéraires
- des questionnaires de lecture
- des résumés

Anouilh
- Antigone

Austen
- Orgueil et Préjugés

Balzac
- Eugénie Grandet
- Le Père Goriot
- Illusions perdues

Barjavel
- La Nuit des temps

Beaumarchais
- Le Mariage de Figaro

Beckett
- En attendant Godot

Breton
- Nadja

Camus
- La Peste
- Les Justes
- L'Étranger

Carrère
- Limonov

Céline
- Voyage au bout de la nuit

Cervantès
- Don Quichotte de la Manche

Chateaubriand
- Mémoires d'outre-tombe

Choderlos de Laclos
- Les Liaisons dangereuses

Chrétien de Troyes
- Yvain ou le Chevalier au lion

Christie
- Dix Petits Nègres

Claudel
- La Petite Fille de Monsieur Linh
- Le Rapport de Brodeck

Coelho
- L'Alchimiste

Conan Doyle
- Le Chien des Baskerville

Dai Sijie
- Balzac et la Petite Tailleuse chinoise

De Gaulle
- Mémoires de guerre III. Le Salut. 1944-1946

De Vigan
- No et moi

Dicker
- La Vérité sur l'affaire Harry Quebert

Diderot
- Supplément au Voyage de Bougainville

Dumas
- Les Trois Mousquetaires

Énard
- Parlez-leur de batailles, de rois et d'éléphants

Ferrari
- Le Sermon sur la chute de Rome

Flaubert
- Madame Bovary

Frank
- Journal d'Anne Frank

Fred Vargas
- Pars vite et reviens tard

Gary
- La Vie devant soi

Gaudé
- La Mort du roi Tsongor
- Le Soleil des Scorta

Gautier
- La Morte amoureuse
- Le Capitaine Fracasse

Gavalda
- 35 kilos d'espoir

Gide
- Les Faux-Monnayeurs

Giono
- Le Grand Troupeau
- Le Hussard sur le toit

Giraudoux
- La guerre de Troie n'aura pas lieu

Golding
- Sa Majesté des Mouches

Grimbert
- Un secret

Hemingway
- Le Vieil Homme et la Mer

Hessel
- Indignez-vous !

Homère
- L'Odyssée

Hugo
- Le Dernier Jour d'un condamné
- Les Misérables
- Notre-Dame de Paris

Huxley
- Le Meilleur des mondes

Ionesco
- Rhinocéros
- La Cantatrice chauve

Jary
- Ubu roi

Jenni
- L'Art français de la guerre

Joffo
- Un sac de billes

Kafka
- La Métamorphose

Kerouac
- Sur la route

Kessel
- Le Lion

Larsson
- Millenium I. Les hommes qui n'aimaient pas les femmes

Le Clézio
- Mondo

Levi
- Si c'est un homme

Levy
- Et si c'était vrai...

Maalouf
- Léon l'Africain

Malraux
- La Condition humaine

Marivaux
- La Double Inconstance
- Le Jeu de l'amour et du hasard

Martinez
- Du domaine des murmures

Maupassant
- Boule de suif
- Le Horla
- Une vie

Mauriac
- Le Nœud de vipères

Mauriac
- Le Sagouin

Mérimée
- Tamango
- Colomba

Merle
- La mort est mon métier

Molière
- Le Misanthrope
- L'Avare
- Le Bourgeois gentilhomme

Montaigne
- Essais

Morpurgo
- Le Roi Arthur

Musset
- Lorenzaccio

Musso
- Que serais-je sans toi ?

Nothomb
- Stupeur et Tremblements

Orwell
- La Ferme des animaux
- 1984

Pagnol
- La Gloire de mon père

Pancol
- Les Yeux jaunes des crocodiles

Pascal
- Pensées

Pennac
- Au bonheur des ogres

Poe
- La Chute de la maison Usher

Proust
- Du côté de chez Swann

Queneau
- Zazie dans le métro

Quignard
- Tous les matins du monde

Rabelais
- Gargantua

Racine
- Andromaque
- Britannicus
- Phèdre

Rousseau
- Confessions

Rostand
- Cyrano de Bergerac

Rowling
- Harry Potter à l'école des sorciers

Saint-Exupéry
- Le Petit Prince
- Vol de nuit

Sartre
- Huis clos
- La Nausée
- Les Mouches

Schlink
- Le Liseur

Schmitt
- La Part de l'autre
- Oscar et la Dame rose

Sepulveda
- Le Vieux qui lisait des romans d'amour

Shakespeare
- Roméo et Juliette

Simenon
- Le Chien jaune

Steeman
- L'Assassin habite au 21

Steinbeck
- Des souris et des hommes

Stendhal
- Le Rouge et le Noir

Stevenson
- L'Île au trésor

Süskind
- Le Parfum

Tolstoï
- Anna Karénine

Tournier
- Vendredi ou la Vie sauvage

Toussaint
- Fuir

Uhlman
- L'Ami retrouvé

Verne
- Le Tour du monde en 80 jours
- Vingt mille lieues sous les mers
- Voyage au centre de la terre

Vian
- L'Écume des jours

Voltaire
- Candide

Wells
- La Guerre des mondes

Yourcenar
- Mémoires d'Hadrien

Zola
- Au bonheur des dames
- L'Assommoir
- Germinal

Zweig
- Le Joueur d'échecs

Et beaucoup d'autres sur lePetitLittéraire.fr

www.lepetitlitteraire.fr

ISBN version imprimée : 978-2-8062-1226-9
ISBN version numérique : 978-2-8062-2057-8
Dépôt légal : D/2013/12.603/144

Printed in France by Amazon
Brétigny-sur-Orge, FR

15097922R00018